BABE RUTH

Troll Associates

BABE RUTH

by Rae Bains

Illustrated by Dick Smolinski

Troll Associates

Library of Congress Cataloging in Publication Data

Bains, Rae.
  Babe Ruth.

  Summary: A brief biography of George Herman Ruth, an
unforgettable baseball player.
    1. Ruth, Babe, 1895-1948—Juvenile literature.
2. Baseball players—United States—Biography—Juvenile
literature. [1. Ruth, Babe, 1895-1948. 2. Baseball
players] I. Smolinski, Dick, ill. II. Title.
GV865.R8B35   1984   796.357′.092′4 [B] [92]   84-2595
ISBN 0-8167-0144-X (lib. bdg.)
ISBN 0-8167-0145-8 (pbk.)

Babe Ruth retired from the game of professional baseball in 1935 and died in 1948. Most of the people alive today never saw the great Babe play baseball. Yet the name of Babe Ruth is as well known today as that of any sports star who ever lived. More than anyone else, Babe Ruth symbolizes the game of baseball.

George Herman Ruth, Babe's real name, was born in Baltimore, Maryland, on February 6, 1895. The Ruth family was poor. Mr. Ruth worked as a horse-cart driver, a salesman, and a bartender.

When George was young, his father and uncle ran a tavern, but it wasn't a very successful business. The Ruth family could not afford a nice home. Mr. and Mrs. Ruth and their eight children had to live in two small rooms behind the tavern.

Mrs. Ruth was often sick during George's childhood, and the children were expected to take care of themselves. Young George, as the oldest child, had a lot of responsibility. He looked after his little brothers and sisters. He also had to sweep up the tavern, wash dishes, and wait on customers.

With nobody to look after him, young George started roaming the streets of Baltimore. He got into all kinds of mischief and caused his family great concern.

Finally, at about the age of eight, he was placed in St. Mary's Industrial School for Boys in Baltimore. St. Mary's, run by monks, was a boarding school for orphaned and delinquent boys. There, young George found the stable and loving environment he needed.

One monk in particular, Brother Matthias, gave special attention to the lonely, confused boy. Brother Matthias was a tall, powerful man whose job at St. Mary's was to keep the youngsters in line. He could be a fearful figure, but he was also a wise, helpful person. It didn't take him long to find the key to helping the young Ruth boy.

It was clear that George Ruth would never be a scholar. But he did show real promise as an athlete. With this in mind, Brother Matthias put George on St. Mary's baseball team and set him on the path he would follow as an adult.

Many years later, Ruth said, "I always felt I could hit the ball, even the first time I held a bat. But Brother Matthias taught me some other things. He made me a pitcher and showed me how to field. He really knew the game of baseball and loved it."

For almost twelve years, St. Mary's was young George's home. And Brother Matthias, on and off the baseball field, was the closest thing George had to a father. He made sure that the boy gave nothing less than his best efforts. By the time Ruth was in his late teens, he was the finest schoolboy ballplayer in Baltimore.

Among George's admirers was Brother Gilbert, the coach of Mount St. Joseph's, a school that played against St. Mary's. Brother Gilbert was very impressed by George's pitching and hitting. In 1914, he recommended the young man to the owner of a professional minor-league team, the Baltimore Orioles.

The team's owner, Jack Dunn, watched Ruth pitch one game and was ready to give him a contract to play for the Orioles. In February 1914, Ruth left St. Mary's for spring-training camp.

For nineteen-year-old George Herman Ruth, the new life in baseball was a wonderful adventure. It was beyond anything he could have imagined. First of all, he had been given five dollars to pay for expenses on the train trip to Fayetteville, North Carolina. That was where the Orioles had their spring-training camp.

George had never had so much money before, and he felt enormously rich. He also found the train ride very exciting. Not only had Ruth never been away from Baltimore before, he'd never been on a train until that day.

The adventure grew even more exciting at the hotel where the team was staying. There was an elevator in the building, and he had never even seen one until then. For hours, George rode up and down, up and down. He even gave the elevator operator one of his precious dollars to be allowed to run the machine.

George was equally thrilled when he went into the dining room and learned that he could order as much food as he wanted at the team's expense. At home, before he went to St. Mary's, there never had been enough to eat. At the hotel, he ate huge meals every chance he got.

George Ruth was thin when he arrived in Fayetteville. But he wasn't thin for long. That spring marked the beginning of an eating style that continued for the rest of George's life.

The young man often topped off an enormous hotel meal with hot dogs and soda at the ballpark, followed by gallons of ice cream and huge chunks of cake. It was as if the poor boy from Baltimore expected to wake up one day and find there was no more food for him. Years later, when he was a wealthy, successful star, Babe Ruth still ate as if each meal might be his last.

Ruth's innocent behavior at his first spring-training camp was amusing to the older players. They teased him about everything. At last, an Oriole coach told the men to stop picking on the kid. The coach warned them, "You be careful with the teasing after Mr. Dunn gets down here. This boy is one of his babes." The nickname "Babe" stuck. He was now Babe Ruth. In fact, the teenager liked his new name so much that he introduced himself that way from then on.

Out on the ball field the young pitcher was more than an innocent kid. He quickly became the star of the Oriole pitching staff. But what surprised everyone even more was Babe's ability to hit the ball often and far. In those days, pitchers were not expected to be good hitters. Babe not only hit well, he hit better than any of his teammates.

Babe was so good that he was bought by
the Boston Red Sox before the season was
half over. The Red Sox were a major-league
team. Babe pitched two games for the Red
Sox, winning one and losing one.

Then he was sent to one of the Red Sox'
minor-league teams, to get more experience

pitching. There, he worked hard to learn as much as he could about the game of baseball. And the hard work paid off. He won so many games that the Red Sox brought him back to the major leagues before the season ended. He was back to stay.

Babe Ruth played for the Boston Red Sox for the next five years. During that time he helped his team win three World Series. But the Babe was more than a fine pitcher. The young left-hander threw a blazing fast ball and a wicked curve ball. After his second full year with the Red Sox, he was voted the best pitcher in the American League.

Yet, as great a pitcher as he was, Babe Ruth was even more spectacular as a hitter.

Baseball fans were delighted by the sight of the big left-handed slugger at bat. In 1918, he hit more home runs than any other player in the American League. Babe was so valuable to the team as a hitter that he often played in the outfield and hit regularly on days when he wasn't pitching. That gave the Red Sox the advantage of his hitting ability on a steady basis.

After the 1919 season, the Red Sox sold Babe's contract to the New York Yankees for a large sum of money. In the fifteen years that Babe Ruth was a New York Yankee, he became a sports legend. Babe drew so many baseball fans into the ballpark that Yankee Stadium, opened in 1923, was called the "House That Ruth Built."

The awesome slugger hit home runs farther and more often than anyone had before him. In one season alone, Babe Ruth hit a total of sixty home runs, and he hit more than fifty homers in three other seasons.

One of Babe's greatest home runs was hit in the 1932 World Series against the Chicago Cubs. It provided one of the most unforgettable moments in baseball history. The Yankees had won the first two games of the series. The third game was played in Wrigley Field, the Cubs' home field. As Babe came to bat in the fifth inning, the Chicago fans began heckling him. So did the Cub players.

Babe didn't say a word as he faced the Chicago pitcher, Charlie Root. After he let the first pitch go by, Ruth held up one finger to signify "strike one." He didn't swing at the second pitch, either. Instead, he held up two fingers—"strike two." Then, Babe stepped away from the plate and pointed at the distant wall of the stadium.

Babe got ready to hit. The pitcher wound up and threw the ball. Babe swung, there was a loud *crack*, and the ball sailed over the outfield wall—exactly where Babe Ruth had pointed! It was an incredibly dramatic moment, and the crowd roared its appreciation.

By the time Babe Ruth ended his baseball career, he had hit 714 home runs and had changed the way the game was played. In fact, almost single-handedly, he made baseball America's number one sport. In doing so, Babe Ruth became one of the most famous people of his time.

Yet, as rich and celebrated as he was, Babe never lost the childlike ways of his youth. To his very last days, he was like a small boy living in a big man's body. He was also very warm-hearted and generous, especially to children, and he was never too busy to sign autographs or visit a young fan in the hospital.

Babe Ruth, who died on August 16, 1948, was one of the first players elected to baseball's Hall of Fame. But he was more than an extraordinary baseball player. He was a symbol of America throughout the world.